IT'S A SHEEP'S LIFE

Grazing in the 23rd Psalm

IT'S A SHEEP'S LIFE

Grazing in the 23rd Psalm

by Mike Nappa

Illustrated by Scott Angle

Standard Publishing
Cincinnati, Ohio

TABLE OF CONTENTS

DEDICATION
For Blake and Kristin Bush. Thanks for loving teenagers. —M.N.

All Scripture quotations, unless otherwise indicated, are taken from the HOLY BIBLE, NEW INTERNATIONAL VERSION®. NIV®. Copyright © 1973, 1978, 1984 by International Bible Society. Used by permission of Zondervan Publishing House. All rights reserved.

Cover Illustration by Scott Angle
Cover design by Dina Sorn
Edited by Tom Finley and Dale Reeves

© 1997 by Mike Nappa
All rights reserved
Printed in the United States of America

The Standard Publishing Company,
Cincinnati, Ohio.
A Division of Standex International Corporation.

04 03 02 01 00 99 98 97

5 4 3 2 1

	How to Use This Book	5
Lesson 1	Can't Find "Shepherd" In the Classifieds Discovering God is our Good Shepherd	9
Lesson 2	Follow the Leader Discovering God's guiding presence in our lives	17
Lesson 3	Shadow Boxing Discovering God's power in the face of obstacles	25
Lesson 4	It's a Big, Big House! Discovering the heavenly home that awaits us	33
Bonus Project	It's a Flock Party! A Saturday afternoon carnival for children —put on by your teenagers!	41

HOW TO USE THIS BOOK

Sasha was six years old when she came to live with the Potters. A victim of abuse and neglect, she was cold, hungry, bruised and full of fear when the authorities found her. Bob and Gayle Potter welcomed Sasha as their own, providing warmth, comfort, food and love.

She was in a new home, but Sasha couldn't forget her past. That became evident when Gayle Potter noticed a trail of coconut shreds leading from the kitchen to Sasha's room. Upon investigation, Gayle found that Sasha had been storing food in her room—under the bed, in the dresser, in the closet, between her mattress and box springs.

In spite of receiving all the food she could eat at meals, Sasha continued to fear for her future. So she did the best thing her six-year-old mind could think of: smuggled food to her room in case she was ever hungry again.[1]

Although they live in near-adult bodies, your students often carry within them the heart of a frightened six-year-old like Sasha. They're scared. They're facing an uncertain future while remembering all too well the scars of their past. They fearfully search for and hoard anything they think will guarantee them safety and comfort—things like popularity, clothes, good grades, jobs, money, cars and good looks.

Christian teenagers don't need to smuggle the scraps this world has to offer—they're living in a new home! Like Sasha, they have someone new to care and provide for them. When teenagers become Christians, they become sheep in the care of the Good Shepherd.

It's a Sheep's Life: Grazing in the 23rd Psalm reintroduces your kids to that loving Shepherd and Overseer of their souls.

Each lesson in this book is divided into three sections: **Open Minds, Open Bibles** and **Open Lives.** Each of these sections presents more than one option for you to choose as learning activities. These are represented by the ♛ icon.

In the **Open Minds** section, you'll find two creative ideas for introducing the topic of the lesson to your youth group. Choose one idea to begin your meeting.

In the **Open Bibles** section, you'll find three activities to choose from that will encourage your kids to innovatively explore selected passages from the 23rd Psalm. The activities in this section are designed to appeal to the different learning styles of your students. Typically, the first suggestion will be the most active, using lots of movement and getting kids out of their chairs. The second, though still active and involving, focuses more on facilitating small group discussions. The third makes use of true-life stories to spark discussion about the Scripture and the topic. You may elect to do one, two or all three of these activities, depending on your time limit and the personality of your group.

In each **Open Lives** section, you'll find two closing activities to help your kids apply and remember what they've learned during your meeting. The first activity uses creative methods to help kids reinforce their understanding and retention of the Scriptures from the lesson. The second activity leads kids in reviewing and applying what they've learned, and offers them a chance to explore more about the 23rd Psalm during the week. Again, select and use the closing that's most appropriate for your group.

Each session includes two reproducible student sheets tied to some of the suggested activities. They are found at the end of each session plan. Photocopy as many as you need for your class, with a few extras for unexpected visitors.

Every session requires paper, pencils or pens and Bibles, so be sure to stock your classroom with plenty of these. Many activities require additional materials such as small prizes, poster board, markers and tape. These items will be listed in the margin.

You'll also notice a few tidbits called **Flock Facts** sprinkled here and there. These provide some fun facts about sheep to tell your kids.

Finally, check out the suggested music ideas also listed in the margin. Music has a way of soothing wild animals—even *your* sheep.

Final Thoughts

I applaud you for choosing to make a difference in the lives of teenagers. And I urge you, as you approach the teaching of this course, to prepare in the following ways:

♛ Pray
E. M. Bounds put it best when he said, "God shapes the world by prayer. The more praying there is in the world, the better the world will be."[2] If you truly believe that God can change your teens' lives through your teaching, then the least you can do is pray for him to do so.

♛ Read the Lesson Ahead of Time
Several activities require minimal preparation, and all activities will go more smoothly if you know what to expect. So invest the time necessary to help familiarize yourself with the lesson.

♛ Trust the Holy Spirit
If I were the greatest writer in the world, and you were the greatest teacher in the world, it still wouldn't be enough to impact your teenagers in the eternal way that only God can. Do your best, but trust God to bring the message home into the hearts of those you teach.

May God bless as you and your teenagers embark on the adventure of *It's a Sheep's Life: Grazing in the 23rd Psalm*.

IT'S A SHEEP'S LIFE

clip-art promo page

Lesson 1

CAN'T FIND "SHEPHERD" IN THE CLASSIFIEDS

Wouldn't it be great if the animal that the Bible used to describe Christians was something impressive like . . . guard dogs? Or tigers? Or even sharks? But that's just not the way it is. Instead of those impressive beasts, Scripture chooses to describe us as sheep—animals especially known for stubbornness, stupidity and helplessness. That's the bad news.

The Bible also tells who our shepherd is—and it's someone more powerful than any guard dog, tiger or shark. Psalm 23:1 reveals, "The LORD is my shepherd." That's the good news—the very, very good news. Because no matter how stubborn, stupid or helpless we are, God is always willing and able to care for our every need.

Use this lesson to encourage your teenagers to place their trust in God, our impressive Good Shepherd.

1 Open Minds

♕ OCCUPATIONAL DESCRIPTIONS

Start this series off with a chance for teenagers to get to know more about each other. Gather everyone in a circle and say, **"Think for a moment about which occupations might best describe you. For example, if your life is characterized by extreme busyness, always rushing from one emergency to the next, the occupation that might describe you could be ambulance driver. Or, if your life is filled with homework, homework and more homework, you might describe yourself as an accountant."**

Give everyone a moment to think, then have group members take turns telling which occupation best describes their lives, and why they chose these occupations. If kids need help, suggest occupations such as teacher, secretary, trash collector, author, nanny, police officer, movie star, cook, social worker, activities director and so on.

After everyone has had an opportunity to share, say something like this: **"The Bible also describes God in terms of an occupation. Psalm 23 tells us that God is a shepherd. For the next few class sessions, we're going to examine Psalm 23 to discover more about what it means to have God for our Shepherd."**

♕ ♕ NAME THAT CREATURE

To begin the lesson, gather everyone together and give each person a pencil and sheet of paper. Then say, **"Let's start off today by**

Lesson Text
Psalm 23:1; Isaiah 53:6; Luke 15:3-7;
John 10:11-14; Romans 8:11-16

Lesson Focus
God is our Good Shepherd.

Lesson Goals
At the end of the lesson, students should:
• Experience tasks a shepherd might perform.
• Discover that God is always on the lookout for his sheep.
• Be encouraged to trust the Good Shepherd to supply all their needs.

Check This . . .
Although it doesn't specifically mention a shepherd, a fun song that reinforces today's message is "Take Me To Your Leader," by the Newsboys. You can find this song on the album of the same name, or on the compilation CD, *Wow 1997: The Year's 30 Top Christian Artists and Songs*.

Materials needed:
Blank paper; pencils

9

playing a game I call 'Name That Creature.' First, number your paper from one to five." (Pause while kids do this.)

"In a moment, I'll begin reading a list of characteristics describing a certain creature. After each characteristic, you may write on your paper one guess of what you think that creature is. However, you get only five guesses total, so choose wisely when to use your guess. Be prepared to select one of your five guesses as your final answer."

When kids understand the rules, begin reading this list:
- THIS CREATURE IS NOT EXTINCT.
- THIS CREATURE HAS NO TOP TEETH.
- THIS CREATURE TRAVELS QUITE A BIT.
- THIS CREATURE IS REALLY QUITE TIMID AND FEARFUL.
- THIS CREATURE IS RARELY ALONE.
- THIS CREATURE ALWAYS LIES DOWN WHEN FINISHED EATING.
- THIS CREATURE IS KNOWN FOR BEING . . . WELL . . . STUPID.
- THIS CREATURE IS ALSO KNOWN FOR BEING . . . WELL . . . STUBBORN.
- THIS CREATURE HAS A BIG, FURRY COAT.
- THIS CREATURE IS TOTALLY DEPENDENT ON ANOTHER FOR ITS SURVIVAL.

Afterward, give kids a moment to select the one guess from their papers that they think is correct. Next, allow several group members an attempt at naming the creature. When it's appropriate, reveal to your students that the creature is actually a sheep.

Then say, **"Even though it's not very flattering, the Bible often describes us as sheep! But that's not all bad. Psalm 23 describes us like sheep, but also reveals that God is our Shepherd. For the next few class sessions, we're going to examine Psalm 23 to discover more about what it means to have God for our Shepherd."**

◆ 2

♕ SHEPHERD TRYOUTS

Begin by saying, **"Let's see how good we are at being shepherds."** Distribute copies of the reproducible student sheet (page 13) to everyone in the group. Comment, **"On this sheet you'll find ten tasks of a normal shepherd. Your job is to complete as many of those tasks as possible within the next two minutes. You must get a witness to initial the appropriate spot to confirm that you've completed a task. Ready? Go!"**

Make a small treat (such as Tootsie Rolls®) available to kids and start timing. Because everyone will be trying to do the tasks at once, there may be a little confusion. If necessary, remind kids they'll need to work with others to complete the most tasks possible.

Give a warning signal when only 30 seconds and only 10 seconds are left. Call time after two minutes, and see who was able to complete the most tasks. Reward that person with a round of applause.

Next, have students form pairs to discuss the questions that follow. After discussing each question for a moment, have pairs report their answers to the rest of the students.

• **What's something new you learned about shepherds through this little tryout?**

• **What would be the best and worst parts of being a shepherd?**

Have one partner in each pair read aloud Psalm 23:1, and have the other partner repeat it in his or her own words. Then have kids continue their discussions with these questions:

• **Why do you suppose God is described as a shepherd in Psalm 23:1?**

Materials needed:
Reproducible student sheet on page 13 of this book; a watch with a second hand; small treats (such as Tootsie Rolls®)

• When have you experienced God's shepherding influence in your life, or when has he shepherded someone you know?
• Why do we need God to be our Good Shepherd?
• Is there something that is keeping you from trusting God to be your Shepherd? If so, what is it? What can you do about that this week?

Conclude this activity by saying, "**Psalm 23 paints a vivid picture of God as our Shepherd, and us as his sheep. Let's dig deeper to discover more about what this means for us.**"

♕ ♕ LOOKING, LOOKING . . .

Gather everyone together and say, "**The Bible makes it clear that God is more than just some run-of-the-mill shepherd. He is our *Good* Shepherd, and because of that, he will always search for his lost sheep. Let's read more about that.**"

Have volunteers read aloud the following Scriptures for the group: Psalm 23:1; Isaiah 53:6; and Luke 15:3-7.

Then have everyone stand while you say, "**Instead of shepherds looking for sheep, we're going to be shepherds looking for something new. Without moving from where you are, take the next few minutes to look around the room and mentally note five things you've never noticed before in here. For example, you might notice a clock, a wall decoration or the color of the carpet. When you've identified five new things, sit down.**"

Wait for two or three minutes, or until everyone sits down. Then let kids share some of the new things they discovered in the room. Next, form groups of no more than four to discuss these questions:
• **What went through your mind while you looked for things you had never noticed before?**
• **What would you imagine goes through God's mind when he notices one of his "sheep" wandering away from him?**

Have groups reread Psalm 23:1 and Luke 15:3-7. Then continue:
• **Why is a shepherd so concerned about sheep who have wandered away? Why does God have a similar concern for us?**
• **When have you felt like a lost sheep?**
• **How does it make you feel to hear that God will always look for you like a shepherd searches for a lost sheep?**
• **Why do people wander away from God? What makes them return?**

Conclude by saying, "**God is our Good Shepherd, and because of that he won't let us wander far before coming to find us. Let's pause for a moment right now to thank him for that.**"

In their groups, have kids pray (silently or aloud) and thank God for being a shepherd who never gives up looking for his sheep. Then move on to the next activity or conclude with **Open Lives**.

♕ ♕ ♕ FEEDING GOD'S SHEEP

After quoting Psalm 23:1 once more, say, "**Just as this verse points out, God has a history of providing all we, his sheep, need. Listen to this true story about a time he did just that.**

"**During the 1800s, George Müller was appalled to see that most of England's orphaned children were left to live in the streets or sent to labor in cruel workhouses. So he did something about it. Müller started an orphanage that eventually filled five houses and cared for 2,000 children at a time. The only problem was how to pay the large expenses for such an orphanage.**

Materials needed:

Bibles

Flock Fact
Whenever a shepherd adds another sheep to the herd, the shepherd puts his or her own unique, lifelong mark on that animal. This is usually a simple design carved right in the sheep's ear. Although this is a painful procedure, it allows shepherds to identify quickly—even at some distance—to whom each sheep belongs.[1] Likewise, the Holy Spirit irrevocably "marks" each of God's sheep with his indwelling presence (see Romans 8:11, 16).

"Still, Müller was always confident that God would supply every need. Whenever there was something the orphanage needed, Müller never asked people for help—he simply prayed and asked God, his Good Shepherd, to provide.

One morning a girl named Abigail visited the orphanage and found a strange sight. All the children were gathered in the dining hall waiting for breakfast to be served. The table was set and everything was ready . . . except there was no food. Müller said to the orphans (and Abigail), 'Children, it will soon be time for school, so let's pray. Dear Father, we thank you for what you are going to give us to eat.'

Almost immediately, there was a knock at the door. It was the baker. 'Mr. Müller,' he said. 'I couldn't sleep last night . . . so I got up at 2:00 A.M. and baked some fresh bread for you.' Moments later, another knock came. It was the milkman. His cart had broken down just outside the orphanage. He had to unload the wagon before he could repair it, and rather than let the milk spoil, he thought the orphanage could use it. Within a few short minutes, God had provided breakfast for all 2,000 children."[2]

Pause for a moment to let the story sink in, then ask, **"What do you think it might have felt like to be one of the orphans in this story? What causes us to mistrust that God will provide for us today? How can remembering Psalm 23:1 and the story of George Müller encourage you to trust God to provide for you this week?"**

Say, **"If God really is our Good Shepherd, then we should be able to recognize his provision for us. So, before we wrap up, take a moment to tell someone near you about a time God provided a need for you or for a person you know."**

3 Open Lives

♛ SCRIPTURE PHOTO FRAMES

Say, **"Let's wrap up today's lesson by creating something to help us remember what we've learned."**

Provide poster board, scissors, magic markers and Bibles. Then invite kids to create photo frames based on today's session. First have students cut out the center of a frame-sized piece of poster board. They may cut an oval, square or any other shape as long as it leaves room for a photograph to be viewed through the opening.

Next, have them write out Psalm 23:1 around the edges of the frame and add any drawings or decorations they like. When everyone is finished, encourage them to take the frames home and tape their photos in it. Ask kids to put these Scripture frames someplace where they'll be reminded daily that God is their Good Shepherd.

Materials needed:
Poster board (or construction paper); scissors; magic markers; Bibles

♛ ♛ REFLECTING ON THE LESSON

Form pairs, and have partners take turns completing the following:
• One important thing I've learned from this lesson is . . .
• One thing I'll do this week to help me apply it is . . .

Distribute copies of the reproducible student sheet on page 15. Comment, **"Use this sheet as a personal Bible study guide sometime during this week to help you learn more about today's topic."**

Use Psalm 23:1 as your closing prayer, having everyone recite it together.

Materials needed:
Reproducible student sheet on page 15 of this book

Shepherd Tryouts

See how many of the shepherd tasks listed below you can complete within the time limit. Have a witness initial each appropriate task to verify you've completed it.

INITIALS   SHEPHERD TASKS

_____   **A SHEPHERD MARKS SHEEP TO DISPLAY OWNERSHIP OF THAT SHEEP.**
"Mark" three people in your group by giving them a high five.

_____   **A SHEPHERD PROVIDES NOURISHMENT FOR SHEEP.**
Deliver a small treat to someone who doesn't have one.

_____   **A SHEPHERD HERDS SHEEP.**
Gather five people into a corner of the room and lead them in shouting, "Sheep Rock!" for ten seconds.

_____   **A SHEPHERD PROTECTS SHEEP.**
Choose one person. Without harming anyone, don't allow others near that person while you count to 10.

_____   **A SHEPHERD LOOKS FOR LOST SHEEP.**
Identify the person farthest away from you, then track down that person and have him or her initial here.

_____   **A SHEPHERD KNOWS EACH SHEEP BY NAME.**
Discover the name of someone you don't know. If you know everyone's name, then discover a person's middle name instead.

_____   **A SHEPHERD CARES FOR BABY LAMBS.**
Find someone younger than you and sing him or her a lullaby. If you're the youngest in the class, sing to your youth leader.

_____   **A SHEPHERD COMBS THE SHEEP'S FUR.**
Brush or comb the hair of a friend. Get permission first! You may use your fingers if no comb or brush is available.

_____   **A SHEPHERD GIVES SHEEP A COMFORTABLE PLACE TO REST.**
Carry a chair to someone and ask him to sit down. If no chair is available, ask someone to sit on your knee.

_____   **A SHEPHERD IDENTIFIES POSITIVE QUALITIES IN SHEEP.**
Tell five people something you like about them.

©1997 by Mike Nappa. Permission is granted to reproduce this page for ministry purposes only—not for resale.

Midweek Explorations from
PSALM 23:1

Something to Read
Take a few moments to reread Psalm 23:1; Isaiah 53:6; and Luke 15:3–7. Next read John 10:11–14.

Something to Think About
After reading the Scriptures above, ask yourself these questions:
• How would I summarize the main message of these verses?
Why is that message important enough to be included in the Bible?

• Exactly what does it mean to me that God is my Shepherd? (Be specific.)

• How will knowing that God is my Shepherd make a difference in my life this week?

Something to Do
Visit a nearby library and check out a book on sheep. (Just a hint: check the children's section. Books there usually focus on only the most important information instead of trying to give an exhaustive look at our furry friends!) Next, look through the book and make a list of at least 10 adjectives used to describe sheep. (Warning: some of those adjectives won't be complimentary!) When your list is ready, read through it and see how many of them might be used to describe you and your relationship with God. Finish off your time by praying that God, the Good Shepherd, will mold you into one of his good sheep.

"The Lord is my shepherd . . ." (Psalm 23:1)

Lesson 1

Lesson 2

FOLLOW THE LEADER

Lesson Text
Psalm 23:1-3; 78:52, 53; Matthew 23:13-17; John 10:2-5

Lesson Focus
God provides a guiding presence in our lives.

Lesson Goals
At the end of the lesson, students should:
• Realize that God's guidance brings real benefits.
• Discover the importance of following God's guidance.
• Commit to following God's guidance this week.

The classic joke goes like this: In 1492 Columbus set sail for the West Indies and ended up in the Americas. That one trip set the precedent for the next 500+ years: Men *still* won't stop for directions.

Although men are the butt of that joke, in reality all of humanity is traveling off course through life. Very few have taken the time to stop and ask the Creator of life for guidance. We prefer instead to trust ourselves, our society, our history, our media, our earthly leaders or a host of other imperfect guides.

Thankfully, it doesn't have to be that way. Use this lesson to help your group members grow in their trust of the Good Shepherd for guidance through each day of their lives.

1 Open Minds

FLOCK RACE

Begin by saying, **"Last time we learned that we are the sheep of a Good Shepherd. Let's begin today by having a flock race!"**

Form four teams. (A team should be at least two people. If you have less than eight students, form only two teams.) Have teammates hook their arms together to create a "flock." Then, without positioning any team at a starting line or identifying a finish line, shout, **"Ready? Go!"**

Wait for kids to respond. Some will take off toward what they think is the finish line. Others will stand around wondering what they're supposed to do. No matter what, don't give kids any guidance for a minute or two. Then gather teams together and have group members answer this question: **"What's wrong with this flock race?"**

Follow up their answers by saying, **"Without rules to guide us, or a leader to tell us what to do, we just can't accomplish what we're supposed to do. It's the same way with sheep. Unless they have a shepherd to guide them, they will wander aimlessly until they either starve or fall prey to predators. Today we're going to learn more about how God can be our Good Shepherd who guides us through each day of our lives."**

♛ ♛ TIC-TAC-TOE GUIDES

Ahead of time, make a copy of the reproducible student sheet on page 21 and cut it apart as indicated. Place each "Encouragement Activity" in its own envelope, and number the envelopes from 1 to 9. Use masking tape to mark out a tic-tac-toe board on the floor of your

> **Check This...**
> Acoustic rockers Brian White and Justice have recorded an excellent song affirming our need to follow God's guidance—no matter where that may take us! That song is "Where You Lead" and can be found on their album, *The Least That I Can Do*. You might consider playing this song along with an encouragement for your teenagers to put the lyrics into action during the upcoming week.

Materials needed:
Masking tape; bean bags; envelopes; reproducible student sheet on page 21 of this book

meeting room. Number each square from 1 to 9.

When it's time to begin, show everyone the nine envelopes and say, **"To begin today's lesson, we need to complete at least five of the activities in these envelopes. The only problem is, we don't have a guide to tell us which activities to use, or in what order to use them. So, we're going to use a tic-tac-toe board to guide us."**

Have kids line up about ten to fifteen feet away from the tic-tac-toe board on the floor. Have the first person in line face away from the board and toss a bean bag over his back toward the board. If it lands in a square, make the corresponding envelope the first of the encouragement activities you perform.

Continue having kids toss the bean bag until it has landed in five separate squares, giving you five different activities to perform. Then have kids complete the activities in the order they were chosen. (Put the bean bag away.)

Conclude by saying, **"Letting a bean bag and tic-tac-toe board guide us in encouragement activities is fine, but in real life we need a guide who is much more reliable. Thankfully, the Bible tells us that God, the most reliable guide of all, will shepherd us through each day. Let's learn more about that right now."**

Open Bibles

♛ BLIND GUIDES

Form pairs. Have kids designate one person in each pair to be a blind guide and the other a treasure seeker. Send all guides to one end of the room, and all treasure seekers to the other. Show everyone a "treasure" (such as a box of doughnuts); also show them a peel-and-stick label or piece of tape.

Materials needed:
A "treasure" (such as doughnuts) for pairs to seek; a small peel-and-stick label or piece of masking tape to use as a marker

Explain, **"I am going to stick this label out of sight somewhere in this room. If you are the first treasure seeker to find it, you will win the treasure for yourself and your partner."**

Have the treasure seekers turn their backs and close their eyes so they can't see where you stick the label or tape. The blind guides are to watch. Then, place the label or tape in a drawer, under a chair or somewhere else completely out of sight.

Tell students, **"Listen carefully to my instructions. Now that I've hidden the label, I want the blind guides to turn around and face the wall. Now I want the treasure seekers to turn around so you can see the room. At my signal, the blind guides are to shout instructions to their partners, telling them where to find the label. However, the guides can only give two kinds of instructions: compass directions and number of paces. For example, you can tell your partner to walk three paces north and six paces west. Anyone who cheats will lose."**

If the blind guides complain that they can't see their partners as they give directions, say, **"That's right—you're blind! However, the treasure seekers can tell their partners where they are. For example, a treasure seeker may shout that he has come to the third chair from the door. The first one to find it is the winner."**

When you give the signal to begin the challenge, chaos will ensue. The more kids in the room, the louder the shouting and the greater the confusion. Listen to make sure no one is giving illegal directions.

After someone has won the treasure, ask, **"Don't you agree that this game would have been much easier if the treasure seekers** had accurate maps to the treasure or the blind guides were able to see and shout out where the treasure was located?"

Read Psalm 23:1-3. Then have pairs discuss these questions:

• **On a scale of 1 to 10, with 10 being best, how would you rate your blind guide's ability to give directions? How would you rate your treasure seeker's ability to follow directions?**

• **In what ways might the green pastures and quiet waters mentioned in Psalm 23 be "treasures" for a sheep?**

• **In what ways is God like a guide for our lives? What "treasures" does he lead us toward?**

• **Have you ever deliberately chosen** *not* **to follow God's guidance in a particular situation? What happened? How might that have been different if you had followed God's guidance?**

• **What do you think Psalm 23:3 means when it says that God guides us in "paths of righteousness"?**

Wrap up this activity by having each pair share insights gained from the discussions. Then say, **"Just as a treasure seeker needs a good map or guide to show where to go, we need a Good Shepherd who'll guide us toward the best that life has for us."**

🐑 🐑 SHEPHERD'S VOICE

Before class, recruit five volunteers to be "shepherd voices." It's best if these volunteers are people not normally associated with your group (so their voices won't be easily recognized), and are either all male or all female. Have your volunteers record the following script on tape.

SHEPHERD #1:	HELLO, EVERYONE! I'M GLAD YOU'RE HERE. FOR THE REST OF THIS ACTIVITY, I WILL BE YOUR GOOD SHEPHERD. DURING THIS TAPE YOU'LL HEAR SEVERAL SHEPHERDS GIVING YOU INSTRUCTIONS. IT'S IMPORTANT THAT YOU RECOGNIZE MY VOICE AND FOLLOW ONLY MY INSTRUCTIONS. READY? LET'S BEGIN.
SHEPHERD #2:	EVERYONE STAND UP, PLEASE.
SHEPHERD #3:	(PAUSE) NO, EVERYONE STAY DOWN.
SHEPHERD #4:	(PAUSE) CLAP REAL LOUD.
SHEPHERD #1:	(PAUSE) BOW YOUR HEADS, PLEASE.
SHEPHERD #5:	(PAUSE) EVERYONE STAND UP, PLEASE.
SHEPHERD #1:	(PAUSE) RAISE YOUR HANDS, PLEASE.
SHEPHERD #4:	(PAUSE) OK, LOWER YOUR HANDS.
SHEPHERD #2:	(PAUSE) OK, LOWER YOUR HANDS.
SHEPHERD #3:	(PAUSE) OK, LOWER YOUR HANDS.
SHEPHERD #1:	(PAUSE) OK, LOWER YOUR HANDS AND RAISE YOUR HEADS. (PAUSE) SHAKE HANDS WITH A FRIEND.
SHEPHERD #5:	(PAUSE) STOP SHAKING HANDS.
SHEPHERD #1:	(PAUSE) STAND ON ONE FOOT.
SHEPHERD #3:	(PAUSE) STOP SHAKING HANDS.
SHEPHERD #1:	(PAUSE) STOP SHAKING HANDS. (PAUSE) LOWER YOUR FOOT.
SHEPHERD #2:	(PAUSE) HOLD YOUR BREATH.
SHEPHERD #4:	(PAUSE) HOLD YOUR BREATH.
SHEPHERD #1:	(PAUSE) HOLD YOUR BREATH. (PAUSE) LET OUT YOUR BREATH.
SHEPHERD #5:	(PAUSE) STAND UP.
SHEPHERD #1:	(PAUSE) KNEEL.
SHEPHERD #3:	(PAUSE) SIT DOWN.
SHEPHERD #1:	(PAUSE) PRAY.

Bring the recording of the shepherds' voices to class. When it's time for this activity, tell kids to pay close attention to the instructions on the

> **Flock Fact**
> Most everyone has heard of sheep dogs, but have you ever heard of a sheep llama? That's right—in addition to training dogs to guide sheep, some shepherds train South American llamas and use them to protect and guide their sheep.[1] Makes you wonder what unusual things our Good Shepherd might use to guide us in life.

Materials needed:
Prerecorded "Shepherd's Voice" skit (see activity); cassette tape player; Bibles

> **Check This...**
> **BAD ADVICE**
> To illustrate the point that we need a shepherd who can help us triumph through our troubles, read aloud this true story:
>
> "Danny Osnato was an aspiring young boxer training for the biggest match of his career. A victory over his next opponent would be an important step toward his goal of being a champion.
>
> As usual, Danny turned to his trainer for guidance in preparing for the big fight. The trainer was confident as he gave this advice, 'Dance the first round out so the other guy can't lay a glove on you. Then, in the second round, come out swinging!'
>
> The day came for the fight. Danny was phenomenal, dancing and weaving exactly as his trainer had guided him in practice. Danny's opponent was stunned and ineffective—he never hit Danny once.
>
> Of course, that really didn't matter. You see, after 47 seconds of fancy footwork, Danny Osnato dropped like a rock to the canvas. He'd passed out from exhaustion.
>
> Danny lost on a Technical Knockout (TKO) in the first round of the bout."[2]
>
> Conclude, "We also need to depend on God's guiding presence in our lives or we risk ending up like Danny Osnato—flat on our backs and down for the count."

Materials needed:
Paper; cellophane tape

Materials needed:
Reproducible student sheet on page 23 of this book

tape, then play it for everyone. If necessary, pause the tape when the shepherds pause to allow kids to respond. If someone reacts to any shepherd besides #1, have that person sit on the floor for the rest of the tape. See how many are able to keep track of the good shepherd's voice and respond accordingly.

Afterward, have everyone join in kneeling and pray: **"Jesus, thank you for being our Good Shepherd. Through this lesson, help us to learn how to recognize your voice each day. Amen."**

For discussion, have kids return to their partners from the previous activity. (If you skipped the previous activity, form new pairs.) Ask:
• **What made it easy or difficult for you to identify and follow the good shepherd's directions?**
• **What makes it easy or difficult for you to identify and follow God's direction for your life?**

Have one partner in each pair read aloud Psalm 23:1-3 and the other partner read John 10:2-5. Ask pairs to discuss these questions:
• **Why do you think the Bible describes us as sheep who need a shepherd to lead us?**
• **If we are sheep, and Jesus is our shepherd, how are we supposed to "hear" his voice?**
• **What can we do when we realize we've followed a poor shepherd like worldly attitudes or sinful desires? How do you think Jesus responds when we do that?**
• **How might your life be different if you really listened to and followed the Good Shepherd's voice during the upcoming week?**

Say, **"We don't have some anonymous and distant shepherd who has left us to make it on our own. We have Jesus, who cares enough to know us and guide us through this life and beyond."**

Open Lives

♛ SHEPHERD SYMBOLS

Tell students, **"As we conclude, let's create something we can take with us to help us share what we've learned."**

Distribute a sheet of paper (or two) to each person, and make cellophane tape available to those who want it. Instruct group members to shape the paper into a "crumple sculpture" that symbolizes for them the message of Psalm 23:2, 3.

Kids may crumple, tear, fold, tape or otherwise shape the paper to create their symbols. For example, they may want to shape their papers into shepherd's staffs, stoplights, cars and so on.

When everyone is ready, let students take turns showing their sculptures and explaining what they symbolize. Afterward, encourage each group member to take home his sculpture and explain it to one person outside the group during the coming week.

Dismiss with prayer.

♛ ♛ REFLECTING ON THE LESSON

Form a circle, and take turns completing these sentences:
• **One thing I discovered during this lesson is . . .**
• **One thing I'll do differently because of this lesson is . . .**

Distribute copies of the reproducible student sheet on page 23. Say, **"Use this sheet as a personal Bible study guide sometime during this week to help you learn more about today's topic."**

Dismiss class with a prayer.

Tic-Tac-Toe Guides

Directions for the leader: Make one photocopy of this sheet to cut apart for use.

ENCOURAGEMENT ACTIVITY #1: Give a 15-second shoulder rub to a friend near you.

ENCOURAGEMENT ACTIVITY #2: Find a partner. Think of three compliments you can give that start with the first letter of your partner's first name and share those with him or her.

ENCOURAGEMENT ACTIVITY #3: Give a 30-second standing ovation to your youth leader.

ENCOURAGEMENT ACTIVITY #4: Tell five people, "I'm glad you're here!"

ENCOURAGEMENT ACTIVITY #5: Find two people who like the same pizza toppings you do, then huddle together and shout, "We're great!"

ENCOURAGEMENT ACTIVITY #6: Take 15 seconds to pray silently for the person nearest you.

ENCOURAGEMENT ACTIVITY #7: All guys must serenade the girls by singing, "For she's a jolly good fellow!"

ENCOURAGEMENT ACTIVITY #8: All girls must serenade the guys by singing, "For he's a jolly good fellow!"

ENCOURAGEMENT ACTIVITY #9: Pat yourself on the back and say, "God loves me!"

©1997 by Mike Nappa. Permission is granted to reproduce this page for ministry purposes only—not for resale.

Lesson 2

Midweek Explorations from
PSALM 23:1-3

Something to Read
Take a few moments to reread Psalm 23:1-3 and John 10:2-5. Next read Psalm 78:52, 53 and Matthew 23:13-17.

Something to Think About
After reading the Scriptures above, ask yourself these questions:
• Who are the guiding influences in my life? Why do I trust them to guide me?

• When have I been under the leadership of a "blind guide" like the ones described in Matthew 23:13-17? What did I learn from that experience?

• Why does God want to be my guide? What would I do if God seemed to be guiding me into a situation or circumstance that made me uncomfortable?

Something to Do
Take a notebook and pencil around with you during a normal day and jot down all of the things you notice that guide you in some way. For example, when you get up, a parent might encourage you to hurry to school. On the way to school you might notice a traffic light, then at lunch time a friend might invite you to join him or her at a certain table. Later, a teacher might show you how to work a math problem or assign English homework.
At the end of the day, look at the list of guiding influences you've made. How many were ones you feel God used to direct you? How many were ones that may have distracted you from God? What's one thing you can you do tomorrow to increase God's guiding influence in your life? Make it a point to do just that.

"He guides me . . ." (Psalm 23:3)

Lesson 2

Lesson 3

SHADOW BOXING

Lesson Text
Psalm 18:1-3; 23:4, 5; 2 Timothy 4:18

Lesson Focus
God provides power in the face of obstacles.

Lesson Goals
At the end of the lesson, students should:
• Compare God's safety to "the world's safest outfit."
• Create a web page based on Psalm 23:4, 5.
• Discuss how God's power can overcome seemingly unstoppable opposition.

This life has a lot in store for your teenagers—unfortunately, much of it is bad. Consider:
• Two-thirds of Americans say they'll "lie when it suits me," meaning your kids are lied to by someone virtually every day.
• Four of every five teenagers in your group will be a victim of violent crime at least once in their lives.
• One of every six teenagers has been a victim of child abuse.[1]

How are your kids to face and overcome these kinds of obstacles? Not by themselves, thankfully. Psalm 23 sounds a cry of hope in the face of difficult times—our Good Shepherd stands close by, keeping a watchful and protective eye on us, his sheep. Use this lesson to plant that hopeful message in the hearts of your teenagers.

1 Open Minds

♛ FEAR-O-METER

Before class, use masking tape to create a "Fear-O-Meter"—a line on the floor marked incrementally (like a ruler) from 1 to 10.

When it's time to begin, have everyone stand at one end of the Fear-O-Meter. Then explain, **"Today we're going to talk about fears. To start off, let's rate our fears on this Fear-O-Meter. I'll read an item, and you rate how afraid of that item you are by standing on the appropriate number on the meter. A '1' means you're not at all afraid, '10' means you're very afraid."**

When kids understand the rules, begin reading items from the list below. Feel free to skip some items or add new ones to make it more appropriate for your group and time constraints. After each item, ask kids to explain what makes that item fearful or not fearful for them, and to tell how they deal with that fear. Encourage them to be honest. If necessary, remind students that put-downs are unacceptable.

HOW AFRAID ARE YOU OF . . .
• DOORKNOBS?
• GOING ON A BLIND DATE?
• SPEAKING IN PUBLIC?
• A BREAKUP IN YOUR FAMILY?
• GOING TO JAIL?
• FIGHTING IN A WAR?
• NEVER GETTING MARRIED?
• FAILING AT SCHOOL?
• DRIVING OVER 100 MILES PER HOUR?
• BEING A VICTIM OF VIOLENT CRIME?
• EATING AN UNKNOWN SUBSTANCE?
• TELLING A STRANGER ABOUT JESUS?
• THE DEATH OF A LOVED ONE?
• BEING RIDICULED FOR YOUR FAITH?
• BEING ABANDONED BY YOUR FRIENDS?
• BEING FORBIDDEN FROM GOING TO CHURCH?

Materials needed:
Masking tape

Check This . . .

For those ska music fans in your youth group, the Supertones' enthusiastic, "Who Can Be Against Me" is a great tune that revels in the comfort from knowing God is on our side. You'll find this song on their album, *Adventures of the O.C. Supertones*. Just for fun, crank this one up and let kids sing along.

If your kids aren't into ska music, you might try Steven Curtis Chapman's pop classic, "King of the Jungle," found on his *Heaven in the Real World* album.

- **GETTING DIVORCED SOMEDAY IN YOUR FUTURE?**
- **A SAFE BEING DROPPED ON YOUR HEAD FROM THE EMPIRE STATE BUILDING?**
- **NOT GETTING A GOOD JOB AFTER YOU GRADUATE?**
- **HELL?**

When it's time to move on, say, **"King David was a man acquainted with fear. For much of his life he was hunted as an outlaw and later was betrayed by his own son. In spite of that, he had great confidence in God's power to overcome any obstacle—and he wrote about it in Psalm 23. Let's take some time now to examine what he had to say."**

Pause for prayer, asking God to direct the learning that takes place.

♛ ♛ MY BUDDY

Follow the directions at the top of the reproducible student sheet (page 29) to prepare your room for this activity.

Materials needed:
Reproducible student sheet on page 29 of this book; writing utensils; scissors; cellophane tape; paper; masking tape

When all have arrived, begin by saying, **"Posted around the room are 10 real-life situations. Your job is simply to decide the one person you'd most like to have with you in each situation. For example, if you were coaching in the Super Bowl, you might want to have the Green Bay Packers' quarterback, Brett Favre, with you. You may choose anyone living or dead to be with you. Write your choice on each sheet of paper. Ready? Go."**

Give kids about 10 minutes to make their choices. Then collect all the situation sheets and gather together for discussion. Read some of the chosen people from each sheet, and ask students to explain why they'd want that person nearby when facing the appropriate situation.

Tell your students, **"King David also faced tough real-life situations. In Psalm 23 he tells us exactly who he wanted with him. Let's take time today to explore what he had to say."**

Pause and ask God to direct the learning that takes place today.

Open Bibles

♛ WORLD'S SAFEST OUTFIT

Form four teams (a "team" can be one person). Give each team a pillow, a cardboard box, a stack of old newspapers, masking tape and scissors. Say, **"In just a moment, your team will have 10 minutes to create 'The World's Safest Outfit' using only the supplies I've given. Be creative, but be prepared to explain how each part of your outfit contributes to the overall safety of the wearer."**

Materials needed:
Four pillows; four cardboard boxes; four stacks of old newspapers; masking tape; scissors; Bibles

When everyone understands the rules, have each team select one person to "model" the outfit, then set kids loose to begin. Encourage group members along the way, and be sure to give them a two-minute warning to let them know when to begin wrapping up.

After all outfits are ready, have models take turns showing off their outfits while other team members explain all the features of their suits. For fun, have kids vote on which suit they think would actually be the safest. Then have kids choose partners from each of the other teams to form new discussion groups of no more than four.

In their foursomes, have kids discuss these questions:

• **What was the biggest challenge for your team while creating your safety outfits? How did you overcome that challenge?**

• **What are some challenges to a person's physical safety in everyday life? What about emotional, intellectual and spiritual safety—what are some of the challenges there?**

• **How do people try to overcome those challenges?**

Make sure each group has a Bible, then have the person wearing the most buttons read aloud Psalm 23:4, 5 for his or her partners. Have foursomes continue discussions with these questions:

26 Lesson 3

- Do you think this Scripture teaches that God will never allow anything to harm us? Why or why not?
- Why could David say with confidence, "I will fear no evil"?
- What was it about God's protection that made David feel safe enough to relax and eat, even in the presence of his enemies?
- How does God provide safety for us today? How does that impact the way you approach obstacles or difficult situations?

Have the person wearing the most brown in each group report any highlights from the group discussions to the class. Then say, "**Just as a shepherd protects his sheep, God exercises protective care over us. That doesn't mean that nothing will ever harm us, but it *does* mean we can turn to him for help with our safety concerns.**"

♕ ♕ PSALM 23 ON THE WORLD WIDE WEB

Form groups of no more than four. Distribute paper and magic markers to each group, and make sure kids have access to a Bible.

Say, "**When we're going through a tough situation, we often forget that God is active in protecting and helping us overcome obstacles. That's when we need the encouragement of Psalm 23:4, 5.**" Pause to have a student read this passage aloud.

Continue, "**Let's take some time right now to think of a way to creatively pass on the encouragement of this passage to others. In your foursomes, imagine that you are a team of expert Internet employees, and your job is to design a brand-new web page based on Psalm 23:4, 5. The page will encourage people to trust God during difficult circumstances. Be as creative as you like, and make it as appealing as possible.**"

If your group is unfamiliar with the Internet, have available a few books about designing web pages. If kids seem stuck, suggest they identify one main theme from the passage, then think of interesting graphics that might illustrate that theme. They can add interactive elements such as a memory verse test or a button that connects the user with a "Psalm 23 Store" that sells memorabilia about these verses. Set a time limit, and make sure they know when time is almost out.

When you're ready, have groups take turns telling about the newly designed web pages. Then have foursomes discuss these questions:

- Judging from what you emphasized in your web page, what would you say is the most important message in Psalm 23:4, 5?
- What difference does that make in your everyday life?
- When are you most likely to forget the encouragement of Psalm 23:4, 5? What can you do about that?
- How might remembering these verses help you the next time you face a difficult situation in life?

Let a volunteer from each group share a response to the last question. Then move on to the next activity.

♕ ♕ ♕ ONE-ON-FIVE BASKETBALL?

Read aloud Psalm 23:4, 5. Say, "**Life is never easy, but in Psalm 23:4, 5 we have a reminder that no matter what we face, God is always on our team. This true story illustrates what that means.**

"Things were looking grim for the senior basketball team at St. Peter's High School. Taking on the sophomores had proved a harder task than expected. One by one, members of the senior team got into foul trouble, and one by one, they began to foul out of the game. All too soon, so many players fouled out that the seniors didn't have enough eligible people to field a full five-man

Materials needed:
Magic markers; drawing paper; Bibles

> **Flock Fact**
> A shepherd's two main tools are a rod and a staff. The rod is a heavy club that's small enough to fit in the shepherd's hand. With hours of practice, the shepherd learns to handle and throw this club to fight off predators wishing to attack the flock. The candy-cane shaped staff is a long, trim walking stick. The shepherd uses this to pull back straying lambs, and also rubs the staff gently on a sheep's side to calm him.[2]

team. No problem, they thought, we'll just play 'em four against five. That worked fine for awhile . . . until another senior player fouled out . . . and another . . . and another.

Finally, with the score tied at 32 and with more than four minutes left in the game, the seniors had only one player still eligible to play because the entire rest of the team had fouled out!

But the seniors weren't worried. Their last player was Pat McGee, and not only was he willing to play one-on-five basketball, he intended to win. Which is exactly what he did.

Over the course of the next four minutes, his suffocating defense didn't allow the opposition to score one point, while his offense added three points to the seniors' score. Because Pat McGee was on their team, the seniors walked away with a 35 to 32 victory over the rival sophomore team."[3]

Afterward, ask:
• **In what ways is life like a one-against-five basketball game?**
• **How is the difference Pat McGee made in the story like the difference God makes in our lives?**
• **How can we help each other, our "teammates" in life, to remember and apply the message of this story and of Psalm 23:4, 5 during the week?**

Say, "**As Psalm 23:4, 5 reminds us, no obstacle is too big for God. As long as we're on his team, the ultimate victory is ours.**"

3 Open Lives

♕ SHADOW SCRIPTURES

Explain, "**We've learned a lot about God's protective presence in our lives, but in spite of that, we've barely glimpsed a shadow of the truth in Psalm 23:4, 5. Let's make something to remind us there is more to learn once we leave here.**"

Materials needed:
White and black construction paper; cellophane tape; markers; Bibles

Distribute a sheet of white construction paper and a sheet of black paper to each person. Have kids think of an image that communicates what they view as the most important thought from Psalm 23:4, 5.

Next, instruct them to use one sheet of paper as a background and tear the other sheet into a "shadow" shape that reflects the image. Have kids tape that shadow image onto the background paper and write "Psalm 23:4, 5" on it as well.

When everyone is finished, encourage students to take their shadow images home and place them in a prominent place.

Dismiss with prayer.

♕ ♕ REFLECTING ON THE LESSON

Have kids think about how they would complete these sentences:
• **As a result of today's lesson, I will . . .**
• **One new idea I gained from today's lesson is . . .**

Materials needed:
Reproducible student sheet on page 31 of this book

If you have time, encourage students to tell two or three people how they completed the sentences. Then distribute copies of the reproducible student sheet on page 31. Say, "**Use this sheet as a personal Bible study guide sometime during this week to help you learn more about today's topic.**"

Dismiss class with prayer.

MY BUDDY

Directions for the leader: Photocopy and cut apart the situations below. Tape each situation to a separate sheet of paper, and post the papers in various places around your meeting room. Make sure you leave room for group members to write on each paper.

Situation 1: You're going on vacation to Disney World.

Situation 2: You're walking to your car late at night in a deserted parking lot.

Situation 3: You just broke up with your boyfriend/girlfriend.

Situation 4: You're facing chemotherapy to treat cancer in your body.

Situation 5: You're interviewing for a job you really want.

Situation 6: You're in charge of teaching chemistry at your school for a week.

Situation 7: You're baby-sitting three preschoolers for a weekend.

Situation 8: You're a witness to a robbery in progress.

Situation 9: You're invited to go on national television and tell the world what it means to be a Christian.

Situation 10: You're meeting with a teacher to protest a bad grade you received.

©1997 by Mike Nappa. Permission is granted to reproduce this page for ministry purposes only—not for resale.

Midweek Explorations from
PSALM 23:4, 5

Something to Read
Take a few moments to reread Psalm 23:4, 5. Next read Psalm 18:1–3 and 2 Timothy 4:18.

Something to Think About
After reading the Scriptures above, ask yourself these questions:
• What's the difference between trusting God to help me overcome difficult circumstances and acting foolishly in the face of danger?

• If God promises to protect us as these Scriptures indicate, then why do Christians still deal with suffering?

• When is a time I've felt God's protection?

Something to Do
Interview five people this week, asking each one the question, "When is a time you've felt God's protection?" Compare their answers with your own and with King David's experience as recorded in Psalms 18 and 23. How are they similar? Different? What do you think God expects from us in regard to his protective care in our lives?

"I will fear no evil . . ." (Psalm 23:4)

©1997 by Mike Nappa. Permission is granted to reproduce this page for ministry purposes only—not for resale.

Lesson 4

It's a Big, Big House!

Lesson Text
Psalm 23:6

Lesson Focus
A heavenly home awaits those who choose to follow the Good Shepherd.

Lesson Goals
At the end of the lesson, students should:
• Discover new ways to spread a bit of Heaven on Earth to others.
• Discuss what Heaven will be like.
• Discover the best thing about Heaven is that Jesus will be there.

Adoniram Judson (1788-1850) pioneered the spread of the gospel message into the Far East, particularly in Burma. But few people know what caused him to find faith in the first place. While staying at an inn for a night, he was placed in a room next to a dying man. All through the night, through the thin walls, he heard cries of terror and despair from the man. Judson could feel the fear in the voice, and was too frightened himself to even go next door to help the man.

The next morning, he discovered two things: 1) the man had died during the night; and 2) he was a college friend of Judson's, an atheist who had refused to believe in God. Witnessing that terror-filled approach to death was enough for Judson to turn his life over to the One who is Lord over Heaven and Hell—Jesus.[1]

Use this lesson to encourage your teenagers to take hope in the Heaven that awaits Christians when this life is over.

1 Open Minds

♛ Searching for Goodness

Begin this activity by saying, **"I have a task for you to start off with—to find a little bit of Heaven here on Earth. I want you to find one thing that reminds you of God's goodness in life. For example, a flower might remind you of the beauty God shares with us, a book might remind you of God's Word or a friend might remind you of God's loyal presence in your life."**

When kids are ready, lead them outside to conduct their search. If necessary, remind them not to disturb any other classes.

When everyone has completed the search, lead kids back to the meeting room. If possible, have them bring their items with them. Once in the room, form a circle and have students take turns showing their items and telling why that reminds them of God's goodness.

Afterward, say, **"In Psalm 23:6, King David reminds us that God's goodness and love provide a little bit of Heaven here on Earth, and that we have a whole lot of Heaven to look forward to in the future. Let's explore more about that today."**

♛ ♛ Taste of Heaven

Begin by distributing a copy of the reproducible student sheet on page 37 to each student. Comment, **"Take a moment now to follow the directions on your paper."**

Check This...
Probably the most popular contemporary song about Heaven is "Big House," by Audio Adrenaline. The rowdy tune and singable lyrics make this a perennial youth group favorite. Play the song (found on the *Don't Censor Me* album) or, better yet, show the appropriate clip from A.A.'s award-winning music video titled (what else?) *Big House*.

Materials needed:
Reproducible student sheet on page 37 of this book; writing utensils

33

Let kids work silently by themselves. After a few minutes, have each person find a partner to form pairs. Have pairs compare what they wrote, then choose one to share with the rest of the class.

When students are ready, have pairs take turns telling everyone the descriptions they chose. Afterward, say something like this: **"In Psalm 23:6, King David described Heaven as the house of the Lord where he would dwell forever. Let's take some time now to explore more about what David had to say."**

♛ BIT-O-HEAVEN INVENTIONS

Materials needed:
Construction toys (such as Legos® or K'Nex®); Bibles

Ahead of time, ask parents of younger children in your congregation to loan you several sets of their kids' construction toys (such as Legos® or K'Nex®). If no construction toys are available, substitute colorful sponges to use as building blocks. (These are available in most discount stores for a nominal price.) If you use sponges, be sure to provide scissors for kids to cut them into "block" shapes.

Form groups of no more than four, and give each group a set of construction toys (or sponges and scissors).

Say, **"Your foursome is a group of genius inventors. Your job is to use your supplies and imagination to create a model of a 'Bit-O-Heaven' machine. You are to invent a machine that will spread a little bit of Heaven all over the world. For example, you may want to create a robot with a gun that 'shoots' smiles, a radar beam that tracks down unhappy people or a radio that always quotes just the right Scripture to encourage people. Use your imagination, work together and have fun."**

Give groups about 10 minutes to invent their machines. Encourage creativity and teamwork, letting them know the sky is the limit.

When they're ready, say, **"It's time for an 'Invention Convention' where we show off our latest creations to the rest of the world!"**

Give each group a few minutes to show off and explain their inventions. Then ask foursomes to discuss these questions:

• **Why do you suppose God allows us to have a little bit of Heaven here on Earth?**

• **What does God use to spread a "Bit-O-Heaven" in your life?**

Have groups read Psalm 23:6, then discuss these questions:

• **How is experiencing God's goodness and love like experiencing a little bit of Heaven here on Earth?**

• **What does it mean to have God's goodness and love follow us each day of our lives? Give an example of what you mean.**

• **What keeps us from recognizing God's goodness and love in our lives? What can we do about that?**

Say, **"Just as David could experience God's goodness and love thousands of years ago, we can also experience his goodness and love today. And when we do, we're getting a little bit of Heaven right here on Earth. Let's stop and thank him for that."**

Form a circle. Have each person think of one thing for which they are thankful which reveals God's goodness and love in this life. For instance, kids might say family, flowers, forgiveness, the Bible and so on. (It's OK if some kids think of the same thing.)

Next, begin a prayer that goes something like this: **"Jesus, thank you so much for shining your goodness and love in our lives through things like . . ."**

Have kids go around the circle taking turns completing the sentence with whatever they thought of, then close by saying, **"Amen!"**

♛ ♛ HEAVENLY TRAVEL BROCHURES

Before this lesson, stop by the office of a travel agent and gather several travel brochures (for a cruise, a beach resort or Disney World, for instance). Bring these to class for reference during this activity.

When ready to begin, form your students into pairs. Give each pair a sheet of construction paper. Make the travel brochures, markers, old magazines, scissors and cellophane tape available to all groups.

Say, **"Now is your chance to practice a new career—travel advertising!"** Show the travel brochures.

"Instead of advertising trips to exotic places on Earth, you're going to create a travel brochure advertising Heaven."

Tell kids they can use any of the supplies you've provided, and suggest they fold the construction paper into the shape of an oversized brochure. Encourage them to look over the travel brochures for ideas, and to try to identify several key "attractions" of Heaven to advertise in their own brochures. Then set them loose with their creativity!

When pairs are finished, have each twosome join with another pair to create foursomes. Have pairs take turns "selling" their heavenly travel brochures to their new partners. Afterward, have the groups read Psalm 23:6 and discuss these questions:

• **What did you decide were the main elements to "advertise" about Heaven in your brochure? Why?**

• **Why do you think David "advertised" Heaven as "the house of the Lord" in Psalm 23:6? What does this imply about what we can expect in Heaven?**

• **How would your life be different if there were no hope of spending eternity with God in Heaven?**

• **What do you think it takes to get to Heaven? Explain.**

• **What can you do this week to prepare for an eternity with God?**

Say something like this: **"As Psalm 23:6 reminds us, Heaven waits for those who trust God to provide it. If you're not sure how to get there, or if you have other questions about how to prepare yourself for an eternity with God, feel free to talk with me later."**

After class, be sure to take time to talk to any who have questions. Be prepared to explain how Jesus' death and resurrection have made it possible for everyone to enter Heaven. Some helpful Scriptures to share are John 3:16; Mark 16:16; Romans 3:10, 23; 6:23; 10:13, 17.

♛ ♛ ♛ HOME

Gather everyone in a circle and read aloud Psalm 23:6. Say, **"Heaven, what David called 'the house of the Lord,' is no fable nor some fairy-tale hope like Santa's workshop. It's a real place that God has prepared for those who trust him, and the best thing about Heaven is that Jesus awaits us there. Here's a true story that shows what I mean.**

"When Wilson was two years old, he was diagnosed as having hemophilia. Two years later, when he was four years old, little Wilson contracted AIDS through an infusion of tainted blood.

By the time he had reached second grade, the disease struck in earnest, causing him to drop out of school and spend the following months in and out of hospitals, frequently experiencing fevers, seizures, internal bleeding and blood transfusions several

Materials needed:
Travel brochures; construction paper; magic markers; old magazines; scissors; cellophane tape; Bibles

Flock Fact

It's during the cold, harsh winter that the shepherd finally brings the sheep back to the home ranch. At the ranch are the shepherd's fields, still waters and a sheltering barn to keep the sheep warm and unharmed from winter storms. After months of traveling through the high tablelands, it's at the shepherd's home where the sheep can finally rest in the safety and security of the place that has been prepared for them.[2]

times a week. Through it all, little Wilson's simple faith in Jesus gave him the courage to keep going.

Then one day, lying in an all-too-familiar hospital bed, Wilson said to his mother fearfully, 'I know I'm dying, but I don't want to leave you yet.' His mother did her best to encourage him, but she knew what he said was true and didn't really know what to say.

Wilson was able to return home for Christmas that year. But on January 12, his mother was forced to bundle him up for one last trip to the hospital. Wilson wouldn't last much longer.

Around 4:45 A.M. the next morning, Wilson suddenly opened his eyes and, with renewed alertness, announced, 'I'm going home, Mom.' Confused, Wilson's mother tried to explain that as long as he was on an IV, they wouldn't be able to go home.

'No, Mom,' he explained. 'I'm mean I'm going home to be with Jesus.' No longer was that fear of dying present, and now Wilson's eyes focused someplace beyond his mother. 'Jesus is coming to get me. Okay, Mom?'

His mother whispered, 'Yes, Wilson.' Fifteen minutes later, he smiled, stopped breathing and walked home with Jesus."[3]

Pause for a moment to let the story sink in. Then have kids each find a partner to discuss these questions:
• Why do you suppose Wilson called his death "going home"?
• If Wilson were here now, what would he tell us about Heaven?
• How will knowing that Jesus awaits us in Heaven affect how you approach life during the coming week? The coming year?

Conclude, "Wilson was only a child, but he knew that Psalm 23:6 was true, and because of that he is right now experiencing the joy of dwelling in the house of the Lord forever."

◆ 3 Open Lives

♕ A PSALM BY ME

Say, "Over the past few sessions we've learned a lot about God and ourselves through Psalm 23. We've seen that God is our Good Shepherd, that his guiding presence is always available, that he can help us overcome any obstacle and that he created Heaven to share with us. As we conclude, let's personalize the message of Psalm 23 into something we can keep for ourselves."

Provide paper and pencils, and make sure Bibles are available. Have teens individually rewrite Psalm 23 verse by verse in their own words. Encourage them to write in a way that is meaningful to them. For instance, an athlete may begin, "The Lord is my Coach . . ."

When everyone is finished, allow a few volunteers to read their new psalms to the class. Then close out the series by having everyone read Psalm 23 aloud as the closing prayer.

♕ ♕ REFLECTING ON THE LESSON

Form a circle, and have kids take turns finishing these sentences:
• One thing from today's study I don't want to forget is . . .
• One way I've changed as a result of this four-meeting series from the 23rd Psalm is . . .

Distribute copies of the reproducible student sheet on page 39 and say, "Use this sheet as a personal Bible study guide sometime during this week to help you learn more about today's topic."

Dismiss class with prayer.

Materials needed:
Paper; writing utensils; Bibles

Materials needed:
Reproducible student sheet on page 39 of this book

Ever wonder how you might describe Heaven if you could use only food for comparisons? Your descriptions might look like this:

If Heaven were an appetizer, it would be <u>Buffalo wings</u> because <u>in Heaven anything is possible!</u>
If Heaven were a dessert, it would be <u>a birthday cake</u> because <u>there's always a reason to celebrate in Heaven!</u>

Now that you've got the idea, it's your turn to describe Heaven using food for comparisons! Write your ideas in the spaces below, and be prepared to share your ideas with someone else.

1. If Heaven were an appetizer, it would be _____ because . . .

2. If Heaven were a pizza, it would be _____ because . . .

3. If Heaven were a vegetarian dish, it would be _____ because . . .

4. If Heaven were an ice cream, it would be _____ because . . .

5. If Heaven were a main dish, it would be _____ because . . .

6. If Heaven were a soup, it would be _____ because . . .

7. If Heaven were a salad, it would be _____ because . . .

8. If Heaven were a fast-food item, it would be _____ because . . .

9. If Heaven were a movie theater concession item, it would be _____ because . . .

10. If Heaven were a dessert, it would be _____ because . . .

Midweek Explorations from
PSALM 23:1-6

Something to Read
Take a few moments to reread Psalm 23:6. Next read all of Psalm 23.
(If you wrote your own version of Psalm 23 during class, reread that as well.)

Something to Think About
After reading the Scriptures above, ask yourself these questions:
• When have I experienced God's goodness and love? Do I have trouble believing that goodness and love will follow me all the days of my life? Why or why not?

• Why do you suppose God created a Heaven where Christians can spend eternity with him? What are you most looking forward to about Heaven?

• If there were no such thing as Heaven, would it still be worthwhile to be a Christian? Explain.

Something to Do
Look back over your "Midweek Explorations from Psalm 23" sheets that you did previously. As you read your thoughts there, what strikes you most? How has studying Psalm 23 made a difference in your life? What do you most want to remember from what you've learned? Take all four of these midweek explorations and put them in an envelope with your name on it. Date the envelope for one year from today, then put it someplace where you'll be sure to see it in a year. Open the envelope then and repeat the instructions in the previous paragraph.

"I will dwell in the house of the Lord forever" (Psalm 23:6)

Bonus Project

It's A Flock Party!

Focus
This is a special event—an afternoon carnival your teenagers plan for the children in your church and community.

After you've finished the four lessons in this book, give your teens a chance to celebrate what they've learned. Let them put on a creative "Flock Party" carnival for the children in your church and community.

Before You Begin

Select a Saturday not long after your four-week session as the day for the carnival. Publicize the date, and make sure your students are aware they'll be putting on the Flock Party during this day. Plan for the carnival to run during the afternoon from around 1:00 P.M. to 4:00 P.M.

One month before the carnival, hold a meeting with your kids to plan the details. Have kids choose refreshment and game booth ideas from those listed below, and brainstorm any other ideas they may want to include in the Flock Party. Remember, your teens are planning a carnival for children, so all ideas need to be aimed at a child's level. Be sure to check out the games below for materials needed.

Create and print plenty of copies of a coupon good for snacks at the refreshment bar or other small prizes. These coupons can be given to children who win games.

Have different kids spearhead different committees, fulfilling the various responsibilities of the carnival. For example, you may want a facilities committee that secures the place for the carnival, a booth construction committee that prepares the facility for use, a refreshment committee that makes sure food and drinks are plentiful, a games committee that prepares and staffs the game booths, a publicity committee that advertises the event and a donations committee that secures needed supplies.

When everyone is sure of their responsibilities, set kids loose to create the carnival. The night before the Flock Party, have everyone join in setting up the facilities. On the day of the carnival, have your teens arrive early for any last-minute preparations, then enjoy the day!

Flock Party Game Booths

1. Lion Whack and Bear Bonk!

Collect enough stuffed animals from the congregation to fill a shelf. Try to get as many stuffed bears and stuffed lions as possible, since those were common enemies of sheep during the time of King

Materials needed:
Stuffed animals (lions and bears); a wooden shelf; concrete blocks; socks

41

David. In the booth, set up the stuffed animals in a row.

Create soft "slingshots" by stuffing one or two socks into the foot of another sock. Make enough slingshots so that children can have three per turn, plus a few extras to keep things moving along quickly.

During the Flock Party, have children take turns trying to throw the slingshots so that they'll knock over the sheep's enemies—the stuffed animals. Award coupons good for a small snack or other small prize to kids who succeed in "whacking" a lion, "bonking" a bear or otherwise knocking over an animal.

◆ 2 Pom-Pom Sheep

Materials needed:
Black felt; black pipe cleaners; white pom-poms; scissors; glue; ruler

Purchase black felt, black chenille wires (pipe cleaners), and white pom-poms at a craft store. You'll also need scissors and white glue. Have your students prepare for this craft by cutting out small triangles of black felt, and cutting the pipe cleaners into lengths of about two inches.

At the booth, help children glue one black triangle onto one white pom-pom as a face. Then have them dip the ends of four pipe cleaners into glue and gently poke these into the pompom as legs. When children are done, they will have a palm-sized sheep.

◆ 3 Can You Shear the Sheep?

Materials needed:
Balloons; disposable razors; whipped cream; rags; paper towels; sheets

Ahead of time, have your teenagers blow up a large batch of balloons. Purchase some inexpensive razors and lots of whipped cream at a local grocery store. During the Flock Party, have teenagers create "sheep" by spreading whipped cream on balloons. Then have teens supervise children as they try to "shear" the sheep by shaving off the whipped cream without popping the balloon.

Warning: This will get messy! Be sure to have damp rags and paper towels nearby to clean up any children who need it. You might also want to drape old bedsheets or plastic over everyone's clothes to protect them from getting too messy.

◆ 4 Hungry Sheep

Materials needed:
Cardboard appliance box; paint; paintbrushes; scissors or razor knife; bean bags; masking tape

Using the cardboard from an appliance box as the canvas, have teenagers with artistic talent paint a large mural with at least three sheep on it. Instruct the artists to paint the sheep with open mouths, and then cut out bean-bag sized holes in the cardboard where the mouths are.

During the Flock Party, allow children to try to "feed the sheep" by tossing bean bags into the sheep's mouths. You may want to make different lines with masking tape, allowing younger children to toss from a closer distance than older children. Give participants three tosses per turn.

◆ 5 Count the Sheep

Materials needed:
Reproducible student sheet on page 45 of this book; scissors; masking tape; sheet; watch; slips of paper; glass jar; prizes

Make enough copies of the reproducible student sheet (page 45) so that you can fill a booth wall with numerous cutout sheep. Then have your teenagers pack that wall with the sheep, making sure that at least some part of each sheep is clearly visible. At the same time, the sheep should be arranged so that it's difficult to quickly count them all. When all is ready, cover the sheep with a curtain or a sheet.

During the Flock Party, have teenagers tell children who visit the booth that they must guess exactly how many sheep are on the wall within a 10-second time limit. Then, periodically, have kids uncover the sheep for 10-second intervals throughout the day. Afterward, have children write their guesses on slips of paper and place them in a jar to be checked later.

Near the end of the day, have your kids check the paper slips to see who came the closest to the right number of sheep on the wall, and award that child a prize (such as a stuffed sheep or small toy). Give small prizes to five others whose guesses were the next closest.

What's a Flock Party Without Food?

Here are some fun refreshment ideas that fit into the Flock Party theme. Encourage your students to add some of their own creative ideas as well. Be sure to label each food and beverage item with the titles below.

1. We Knew You Were Coming, So We Baked a (Sheep) Cake

Have your teenagers prepare cakes decorated as sheep. For each "sheep cake," instruct kids to bake one large round cake (for the torso) and one smaller round cake (for the head). Arrange the cakes next to each other to create the appropriate body shape, then use white frosting shaped into curlicues to look like wool. Add black licorice bits to create eyes, nose and a mouth. For even "furrier" sheep, sprinkle coconut over the top. For individual cake treats, consider using a cupcake for the torso and a mini-muffin for the head.

2. Veggie Pastures

For those health-conscious eaters, create several vegetable trays and label them "Veggie Pastures." Include plenty of green vegetables such as celery sticks, green pepper strips and broccoli spears, as well as traditional treats like carrots and mini-corn cobs.

3. Greener Pastures

Offer children a choice of gelatin "jigglers" (all green, of course). Use molds to make a variety of fun shapes, and spread them out over a tray or cookie sheet to create a "green pasture" for children to graze at during the Flock Party.

4. Shepherd Staffs

Have kids purchase breadstick dough from a local grocery—it comes in a cardboard tube like cookie dough. Shape the dough into dozens of shepherd staffs before baking. Leave some plain, add salt to others to create a giant pretzel-type snack and baste a few others with garlic butter.

Check This...

If your teens are energized by creating this fun experience for children, encourage them to put on more parties for the children's ministry in your church. A few helpful resources they might consult are Children's Ministry Parties and Carnivals, by Susan L. Lingo (Group Publishing) and The Big Book of Theme Parties, Snacks and Games for Kids! (Gospel Light).

5. Still Waters

After children have worked up a thirst at the game booths, they'll want something to drink. If your Flock Party takes place during a warm season, fill a large punch bowl with blue Kool-Aid® and call it a "pool of still water" for thirsty sheep. For extra fun, drop in ice cubes and tell everyone they're little sheep swimming in the pool!

If your Flock Party takes place during a cold season, make a big pan of hot chocolate and serve it with marshmallows. Tell kids the marshmallows are little sheep caught in a "mud bog."

Count the Sheep

Photocopy and cut out many copies of these sheep for use in the "Count the Sheep!" game booth.

©1997 by Mike Nappa. Permission is granted to reproduce this page for ministry purposes only—not for resale.

Bonus Project

NOTES

Introduction

[1] Ron Mehl, <u>The Cure for a Troubled Heart</u> (Sisters, OR: Multnomah Books, 1996), pp. 68, 69.

[2] Mike and Amy Nappa, <u>52 Fun Family Prayer Adventures</u> (Minneapolis, MN: Augsburg Books, 1996), p. 29. First quoted from <u>Purpose in Prayer</u>, by E. M. Bounds.

Lesson 1

[1] Philip Keller, <u>A Shepherd Looks at the 23rd Psalm</u> (New York: HarperPaperbacks, 1970), p. 10.

[2] Dave and Neta Jackson, <u>Hero Tales</u> (Minneapolis, MN: Bethany House Publishers, 1996), pp. 105-108.

Lesson 2

[1] Dorothy Hinshaw Patent, <u>The Sheep Book</u> (New York: Dodd, Mead and Company, 1985), p. 40.

[2] Ross and Kathryn Petras, <u>The 176 Stupidest Things Ever Done</u> (New York: Main Street Books/Doubleday, 1996), p. 19.

Lesson 3

[1] Mike Nappa, Amy Nappa and Michael Warden, <u>Get Real: Making Core Christian Beliefs Relevant to Teenagers</u> (Loveland, CO: Group Publishing, Inc.), pp. 41, 42, 86.

[2] David & Helen Haidle, <u>He Is My Shepherd</u> (Portland, OR: Multnomah, 1989), pp. 12-17.

[3] <u>The Boy Who Sold 10 Million Crickets and Other Crazy Facts About People</u> (New York: Parachute Press, Inc., 1991), p. 12.

Lesson 4

[1] E. Myers Harrison, "The Conversion of Adoniram Judson," printed in <u>The Moral of the Story</u>, compiled and edited by Jerry Newcombe (Nashville, TN: Broadman & Holman, 1996), pp. 351-353.

[2] Philip Keller, <u>A Shepherd Looks at the 23rd Psalm</u> (New York: HarperPaperbacks, 1970), p. 136.

[3] Denise Wicks-Harris, "The Courage Not to Fight," printed in <u>A Third Serving of Chicken Soup for the Soul</u>, by Jack Canfield and Mark Victor Hansen (Deerfield Beach, FL: Health Communications, Inc., 1996), pp. 170-175.

Other Empowered Youth Products from Standard Publishing

FOR GUYS ONLY
Young Men Behaving Godly

By Michael Kast

A four-session elective for junior-high and senior-high guys that will really get them thinking about what it takes to be a real man of God. A bonus event includes manly games and activities. Includes reproducible student sheets, numerous options and suggestions for using contemporary Christian music.
Order number 26-23307 (ISBN 0-7847-0737-5)

FOR GIRLS ONLY
Fearless and Female for God

By Jane Vogel

This four-session elective for junior-high and senior-high girls deals with God's plan for them to be both strong and gentle. A bonus girls-only sleepover is included, as well as reproducible sheets, open-ended questions for in-depth discussion, flexible learning activities and contemporary music suggestions.
Order number 26-23308 (ISBN 0-7847-0738-3)

THE BIG GULP
The Adventures of a Reluctant Missionary
A creative study of the book of Jonah

By Rick Bundschuh
Four sessions designed to help senior-high teens grapple with the tough assignments God has given them. Also includes a bonus outreach event. Two reproducible student sheets per lesson, contemporary Christian music suggestions and more options than you could possibly use!
Order number 26-23306 (ISBN 0-7847-0736-7)

CLUELESS EVANGELISM:
How to Share Your Faith When You Haven't Got a Clue

By Michael Kast

A four-session elective for junior-high students (plus a bonus session that is an outreach event). The "kids reaching kids" strategy really works without coercing students to share their faith. Includes reproducible student sheets, numerous options and suggestions for using contemporary Christian music.
Order number 26-23302 (ISBN 0-7847-0612-3)

To order, contact your local Christian bookstore.
(If the book is out of stock, you can order by calling 1-800-543-1353.)